THE EARLIEST SOURCES FOR THE LIFE OF JESUS

BY

F. CRAWFORD BURKITT, M. A., D. D.

NORRISIAN PROFESSOR OF DIVINITY IN THE
UNIVERSITY OF CAMBRIDGE, ENGLAND

Wipf & Stock
PUBLISHERS
Eugene, Oregon

Wipf and Stock Publishers
199 W 8th Ave, Suite 3
Eugene, OR 97401

The Earliest Sources for the Life of Jesus
By Burkitt, F. Crawford
ISBN: 1-59752-184-1
Publication date 5/10/2005
Previously published by Houghton Mifflin Company, 1910

CONTENTS

CONTENTS

THE EARLIEST SOURCES FOR THE LIFE OF JESUS

I

PRELIMINARY CONSIDERATIONS

"THE originator of that name," — Tacitus is speaking of those whom the common people in Rome, as he says, called "Christians" as a term of reproach, — "the originator of that name, one Christus, had been executed in the reign of Tiberius by order of the Administrator, Pontius Pilate." The contemptuous sentence of the Roman historian[1] is the only information about the life and career of Jesus of Nazareth that has come down to us independently of Christian tradition. So far as it goes, however, it agrees with what we read in the Gospels: Pontius Pilate occupies in the statement

[1] *Annals*, xv. 44.

of Tacitus the same place that he occupies in the Church's Creed. He stands there to mark the date of the Crucifixion.

The Christian Church grew up in obscurity under conditions that were by no means favourable to the preservation of accurate historical reminiscences of its earliest beginnings. By the time the Christians began to preserve in writing the record of the origin of their religion, deep and ever-widening gulfs had intervened between them and the events. Jesus was born a Jew, and he lived and died among his own countrymen in Palestine; his religion took root in the great cities on the eastern half of the Mediterranean. The first disciples, the men who had really known the Master according to the flesh, were Aramaic-speaking Semites; in a couple of generations the great majority of Christians were Greek-speaking townsfolk, mixed perhaps in blood, but educated wholly in Greek ways of thought. In the interval the Jewish State had been annihilated by the forces of the Roman Empire, and what remained of the earliest community of disciples had been broken up.

But the cause that most of all tended to make the Christians careless of preserving the memory of the past was that their minds were set upon the future, the future which they believed was immediately in store for them and for all the world. They, the first Christian converts, had obeyed the call to save themselves from the crooked generation of their contemporaries.[1] They had turned from idols to serve a living and true God and to wait for His Son from heaven, whom He raised from the dead, even Jesus, their deliverer from the wrath to come.[2] That generation, some of them at least, would not taste of death till they saw the Kingdom of God come.[3] Jesus their Lord

[1] Acts ii. 40. [2] I Thess. i. 9. [3] Mark ix. 1, and parallels.

was not only the Faithful Witness, the First-born of the dead; "behold," they said, "he cometh with the clouds; and every eye shall see him, and they also which pierced him; all the tribes of the earth shall mourn over him." [1]

The time was at hand — the time of the judgment of the heathen and the vindication of the Saints. What was the use of looking back to the humble life of the Son of God on earth, save perhaps to record his final victory over death, which was the earnest and prelude of his immediately expected Presence in glory? In the events of his earthly career the believers took little interest: if they looked back at all, it was to declare that the Lord himself had instituted the rite of the common meal for which they met week by week, and that he had prescribed the form of their daily prayer to their Father in Heaven. This is no fancy picture.

[1] Rev. i. 7.

It reflects the general attitude of Christians towards the life of Jesus on earth, which we can gather from monuments of early Christianity so representative and so different from one another as the New Testament epistles and the ancient Christian manual known as the "Didache."

The New Age came in a form very different from what had been so confidently expected. The little companies of believers did not live to see their Lord appear visibly on the clouds of heaven. Instead of being caught up alive in clouds to meet the Lord in the air,[1] they went one by one to their graves, leaving their successors to carry on the work and the traditions of the Christian Society. Naturally the changed conditions reacted upon Christian theology, upon the Christian view of the Church and of the dispensation in which it found itself. St. Paul himself seems to have been the first

[1] I Thess. iv. 17.

to realize the new world. He learned to see in the Death of the Christ not merely the last act, the last catastrophe of the old dispensation, but also a process which the individual believer had mystically to undergo on earth, so that the historical event of the Crucifixion remained an ever-present reality to the members of the Christian community.[1]

"Crucified under Pontius Pilate"—in this phrase we see the indispensable germ of history in the Christian Creed. As the believers meditated yet further upon the nature of their Lord, they perceived that he was no chance favourite of Heaven, but one who had been destined to fulfil his high career in the fulness of time. The Church was the inheritor of the promises made to the fathers of old; it hardly needed tradition for them to believe that the Lord Jesus had come of the seed of David ac-

[1] See Rom. vi. 3–6; Col. i. 12 ff.

cording to the Scriptures. At the same time both their own devotion, and the doctrine of such Jewish books as the Book of Enoch, assured them that the Elect One had existed from the first with the Most High. It is not surprising to find that there grew up a belief that his birth was miraculous, shewing that he was in some sense both God and man. The statements about Jesus Christ which we find in the Creed are such as might have been anticipated.

It is also not very surprising that at length a book should have been written which professes to give an account of the earthly doings and sayings of the Lord, which, setting forth from his eternal preexistence with the Father, declares his claims to divine authority, exhibits his unbounded power over disease, over nature, and over death itself, and then goes on to relate how he voluntarily gave himself up to be crucified, and, when all was finished, tells how he appeared to his faithful friends and disciples; a book written that the readers might believe that Jesus is the Christ, and that believing they might have life in his name.[1] Such a book as the Gospel according to Saint John we might expect to spring up within the Church and be accepted as the official account of the Incarnation of the Son of God.

I have begun this discussion of the earliest historical sources for the life of Jesus with the "Apostles' Creed" and the Fourth Gospel rather than with the documents that modern criticism regards as giving us materials for history, because I venture to think that the first thing needed to enable the modern investigator to judge the surviving documents aright is the attempt to look at them rather from the point of view of the early Christians than from that of our own aims and desires. It is sometimes

[1] John xx. 21.

felt to be a matter of surprise or regret that modern investigators of the Gospel History reject so much of the traditional matter as unhistorical; it is regarded as a matter of surprise or regret that so small an amount of the "Gospels," canonical or uncanonical, is found to come up to our modern standard of what history should be. Closely connected with this feeling is the vague expectation that the spade of the explorer in Egypt or Palestine will some day dig up something of revolutionary importance, something that will let us go, so to speak, behind the scenes of the rise of Christianity. This expectation has been doomed again and again to disappointment, interesting as the discoveries of the last fifty years have been to those who know within what limits we may hope to gain accessions to our knowledge. It is unlikely that such a revolutionary document ever existed, or, if it ever existed, that it would have been copied and preserved. There were no disinterested observers of early Christianity. Those who did not "believe" had no reason for analysing the elements of what must have seemed to them to be a new and vulgar superstition; so that our knowledge of it comes exclusively from the works of already convinced Christians. The question that the scientific investigator has to ask is not why so much of our material seems to be, strictly speaking, unhistorical, but how it comes to pass that any real historical memory of Jesus Christ was preserved. It is easy enough to explain the genesis of the Creed, and the existence and general scope of such a document as the Fourth Gospel. The real problem is the survival of the Gospel according to Mark.

The difference of standpoint between the ancient and modern world that is clearly apprehended by all reflecting persons at the present day concerns the course of

Nature and the domain of Physical Science. We all of us have some idea of the observed uniformity of nature, and we regard what are called "miracles" as at least unlikely, even if we do not regard them as impossible. Now it is quite evident that the early Christians did not regard "miracles" as unlikely, in the sense that we regard them as unlikely. The Gospels, and many other early Christian documents, are full of miracles, and in some quarters this raises a prejudice against them, or at least against the stories which contain a "miraculous" element. On the other hand, there are no miracles in the "Sermon on the Mount," or in the fragmentary document dug up a few years ago at Oxyrhynchus in Egypt, and commonly called "Sayings of Jesus"; such pieces of tradition as these are often therefore accepted with little or no serious criticism as being genuine and authentic, merely because they claim to be so. But this is fundamentally unscientific. It is of course logical enough for the thoroughgoing traditionalist to accept the "Sermon on the Mount" as genuine and authentic, because it is part of the authoritative tradition of the Church, and to look with very great suspicion upon the Oxyrhynchus "Sayings," because they were not included in the Church's tradition. But those who feel themselves free to criticise the Gospel miracles are bound to examine the credentials of the Gospel Sayings.

A truly scientific historical criticism is both stricter and more catholic than popular liberalism. It does not expect from any document an impossible standard of truthfulness and accuracy. Even the modern astronomer in a scientific observatory has his irreducible personal equation; even the actual eye-witness will tell his tale with variations after the lapse of a few years. Even if we incline to disbelieve in miraculous interference with the course of nature, that does not mean that we have any right to treat stories which contain a miraculous element as if they were mere free inventions. The real question that must be asked is, in the first place, one of origin rather than of faithfulness.

It may not be out of place, before examining the Synoptic Gospels and other parts of the tradition in detail, to consider some of the marks and signs that do indicate that a tradition or saying is really in touch with the events of the life of Jesus of Nazareth. When we consider that our documents are Greek and that the original public for whom they were prepared were Greek-speaking Christians in the cities upon or near the shores of the Mediterranean, it is obvious that what we are looking for are signs which indicate a real knowledge of the conditions of life in Palestine among the Jewish people during the first half of the first century A. D. These signs may conveniently be grouped under the heads of (1) Jewish Topography, (2) Jewish Language, (3) Jewish Thought.

1. *Jewish (and Palestinian) Topography.*—As compared with the ignorance of topography displayed in most of the apocryphal Acts of the Apostles, it is reassuring to note the general correctness of the geographical information given in our Gospels, not excepting the Fourth Gospel. Most of the places mentioned in the Gospels can be identified, or are mentioned in purely Jewish documents such as the Talmud. When we find in words ascribed to Jesus references to Chorazin and Capernaum,[1] towns not mentioned in the Old Testament, though their existence is attested in the Talmud, we may infer that we are dealing with a Palestinian tradition. The Gospel tradition

[1] More accurately, Capharnaum.

never makes Jesus have anything to do with the heathen and Greek-speaking cities of Palestine. He never is made to go to Cæsarea. Peter's confession is not at Cæsarea Philippi: Jesus is with his disciples "in the villages of Cæsarea Philippi,"[1] i. e. in the native suburbs or districts round the new heathenish city. Tiberias, founded A. D. 26 and afterwards the centre of Jewish life in Galilee, is only mentioned once and that incidentally;[2] and we actually know from Josephus that Herod's newly built town was regarded at first with disfavour by the Jews. Of course, correctness and appropriateness in geographical names do not necessarily imply the historicity and accuracy of the stories in which they occur. But such things do shew that the tradition has roots in the soil of the Holy Land.

We must, however, distinguish this real geographical knowledge from a geograph-

[1] Mark viii. 27. [2] John vi. 23.

ical knowledge which is only the result of studying the Old Testament or some other literary source. Both kinds of knowledge may be notably illustrated from the writings of Luke. St. Luke is at home in Asia Minor and on the sea. The narrative portion of the twentieth chapter of Acts is full and correct enough for a guide-book, and the voyage of Paul, with the shipwreck, reads like what no doubt it really is, an account written by an eye-witness. But when the same author is writing of Palestine, he is merely well read, and like other merely well-read persons he occasionally falls into error. He is careful indeed of his language, and talks of the "Lake," not the "Sea," of Gennesareth;[1] but all the Jews' country is often loosely called "Judæa" by him[2] in a way that betrays a foreigner's hand, while some of his statements in Luke iii. 1 and

[1] Contrast Luke viii. 23 ff. with Mark v. 1.

[2] Luke i. 5; iv. 44; vii. 17.

Acts v. 36, 37, seem to rest upon a careless use of Josephus. It is therefore unjustifiable to press Luke's proved accuracy with regard to the conditions of society in Asia Minor as an argument for the accuracy of his knowledge of Palestine.

The apocryphal Gospels shew less knowledge of Palestine than the canonical Four. This is the case even with the fragment discovered at Oxyrhynchus in 1905, which at first was supposed to exhibit a real acquaintance with Jerusalemite ritual and topography. Further investigation, however, seems to shew that the writer's ideas of the topography of Jerusalem were derived from the Old Testament in Greek, and that his ideas of Temple ritual imply familiarity with Egyptian rather than with Jewish customs.[1] If that be the case, the sayings ascribed in the fragment to Jesus are more

[1] See H. B. Swete, *Zwei neue Evangelienfragmente*, in Lietzmann's *Kleine Texte*.

likely to represent the ideas of some Egyptian Christians of the second or third century, than to be based upon what Jesus really said in Palestine in the first century.

2. *Jewish Language.* — In some of our documents, and notably in the Gospel according to Mark, we actually find words and sentences written down in Jewish Aramaic, the vernacular of Palestine. Words like *Abba* (i. e. "My Father"), and the cry "Eli, Eli, lama sabachthani," on the Cross, could not have been invented by Greek-speaking persons. They must have come down to us direct and unchanged from the living memory of the first Palestinian disciples. The solemn "Amen" at the beginning of our Lord's sayings, unfortunately translated in English and turned into "Verily," is another instance of direct reminiscence of his manner of speech. For the most part these Semitic phrases tend to be left out in the later documents, and

in one case a non-canonical document, the Gospel of Peter, has actually transmitted a mistranslation of the foreign word. But the fact that such words occur in any of our documents, and that they have not been altogether distorted in transmission, is a very strong indication that such documents contain a historical element not very far removed from the actual events.

Direct transliterations of Semitic words and phrases are, after all, a sort of historical luxury beyond what one has a right to demand. Almost equally conclusive, if not quite so dramatically telling, are the Aramaic idioms scattered over the Gospels, especially in the recorded words of Jesus. Take, for instance, the use of the word *homologîn*, translated "confess." In Matthew vii. 23 it is used merely of a solemn asseveration; in Matthew x. 32, and in some other places, it is used most curiously with the preposition "in." Jesus says, "those who *confess in* me, I will *confess in* them," meaning that those who acknowledge that they are his disciples, he will acknowledge to be his disciples. This is mere Aramaic idiom taken over into Greek, shewing that the saying itself must have been originally uttered in Aramaic, and that its Greek form is an almost literal translation of the original.[1] It may in fact be said, that, if we are to regard any alleged saying of Jesus as genuine and historical, we must be able to put back its essential terms from the transmitted Greek into the original Aramaic.

Equally searching are the arguments to be derived from the Old Testament quotations and allusions in the Gospel. If they depend upon the renderings of the Septuagint, they are suspect; if they be genuine, they will be independent of the Septuagint, and will imply a direct use of the Hebrew

[1] It is curious that the idiom does not appear in Greek with the verb for "deny."

original or of the Aramaic Targum. This is so important a point, that it may be worth while to explain it more fully. The Septuagint is the name commonly given to the ancient translation into Greek of the Hebrew Pentateuch and other Jewish Scriptures, made at Alexandria in the time of the Ptolemies. This version had become the Bible of the Greek-speaking Jews in New Testament times, and from them it passed over to the Christians. In essentials, apart from corruptions of text and certain substitutions in the less-read books, it became the Bible of the Church, and it is the Bible of the Greek Church still. It was therefore through the Septuagint, and through the Septuagint alone, that the Bible was known to Christians during the second century and the latter part of the first century, i. e. during the time that our Gospels assumed their final shape and became canonical. The original Hebrew was a sealed book to them after the Church had definitely separated from the Synagogue, i. e. ever since the great catastrophe of 70 A. D. A man like St. Paul could use the Scriptures both in Hebrew and in Greek. He had had some regular Rabbinical training, and he quotes the Bible like a modern English scholar who can read his Greek Testament and who gives sometimes the renderings of the ordinary English version, sometimes his own renderings direct from the original. But our Lord and his first disciples spoke Aramaic; there is nothing to suggest that they were acquainted with the current Greek version. In the Synagogues they would hear the Scriptures read in the original Hebrew, followed by a more or less stereotyped rendering into the Aramaic of Palestine, the language of the country, itself a cousin of Hebrew. A faithfully reported saying therefore of Jesus or of Peter ought to agree with the Hebrew against the Greek, or at least ought not to acquire its point and appropriateness from a peculiar rendering in the Greek.

A couple of examples will illustrate what has been said. The Gospel of Matthew alone records the circumstance that Jesus used to quote the word of the Lord by Hosea, "I desire mercy and not sacrifice."[1] It is a point in favour of the authenticity of the saying that it agrees with the Hebrew text against the Greek translation of the Prophets, which had "I desire mercy *rather than* sacrifice." At least, it shews us that the tradition about this saying of Jesus goes back to a Palestinian source. We may take as a contrast the story told in Matthew xxi. 16, and there only, that when the boys were crying out "Hosanna" in the Temple, and the Chief Priests were vexed, Jesus replied, "Have ye never read, 'Out of the mouth of babes and sucklings

[1] Hosea vi. 6.

thou hast perfected *praise?*'" Here the whole point of the saying is in the word 'praise,' but it is a word that does not occur in the original Hebrew at all. In the Hebrew of Psalm viii. 2 we find, "Thou hast ordained *strength*"; it is only in the not very accurate Greek translation of the Psalms that "praise" occurs. The story therefore has evidently at least been recast by some one who used the Old Testament in Greek, and we must consider it improbable that Jesus really quoted this verse from the Psalms in the circumstances alleged.

Both the above instances are taken from the Gospel according to Matthew. The compiler of that Gospel gives the quotations from the Old Testament which he makes in his own person sometimes direct from the Hebrew, sometimes according to the current Greek translation. Like Paul of Tarsus, he illustrates in himself the transplantation of the Christian movement from the Semitic soil in which it germinated into the Græco-Roman civilization. Luke, on the other hand, always uses the Septuagint in his own quotations and allusions to the Old Testament. Whether he was able to understand any Semitic language is of course unknown to us; but his acquaintance with the Bible is certainly derived from the Greek. We cannot, therefore, believe that he gives us the actual words used by Jesus in the Synagogue at Nazareth;[1] for the passages there quoted from Isaiah lxi. 1 ff. and lviii. 6 are taken from the Septuagint. But the quotation from Isaiah liii. 12, at the end of the sayings given in Luke xxii. 35–37, sayings which on general grounds appear to have the ring of genuineness, does not agree in diction with the Septuagint and does agree with the Hebrew. Here, therefore, we

[1] Luke iv. 18 ff.

have an instance of faithful reminiscence of our Lord's words.

3. *Jewish Thought.*—Properly to discuss the Jewish thought expressed and presupposed in the Gospels would be to write a full commentary on them. For our immediate purpose it will be sufficient to point out that hardly any other kind of thought is presupposed. There is no doubt a certain amount of thought and philosophy which is ultimately Greek, whatever be its immediate origin, presupposed in the Fourth Gospel. In the Nativity Stories, also, some critics have seen Greek notions underlying the narrative. But it is the obvious fact that in the rest of the Gospels the Greek influence, so far as the thought and mental atmosphere of the subject-matter are concerned, is simply non-existent. Apart from questions of language and purely literary criticism, the three Synoptic Gospels might be translations from the

Aramaic. The main ideas of the Synoptic Gospels, the fundamental phrases round which move the thoughts belonging to the Gospel, all have their explanation and illustration from contemporary Judaism. The Kingdom of God, the Christ or Messiah, the Day of Judgment, treasure in heaven, Abraham's bosom,—all these are Jewish ideas, entirely foreign to the native thought of the Græco-Roman world. We hear nothing in the Gospels about the Immortality of the Soul, much about the Resurrection at the last day; nothing about "Virtue," much about "Righteousness," little about Purification, much about the Forgiveness of Sin. Even the polemic against heathenism is absent.

To such an extent are the Synoptic Gospels Jewish books, occupied with problems belonging originally to first-century Judaism, that it makes large parts of them difficult to use as books of universal religion.

But it is just this Jewish character that gives them their value as historical documents. "Lo! the Kingdom of God is in your midst!" said Jesus once. The Oxyrhynchus "Sayings of Jesus," representing a development of Christianity among the Greek-speaking townsfolk of Egypt, combines this phrase with the old Greek Delphic precept "Know thyself!" If the saying had been transmitted to us only in this connexion, we might well hesitate to receive it as a genuine utterance of Jesus of Nazareth. But the canonical Gospel of Luke joins it with the announcement of the unexpected advent of the Kingdom of God, which would come before those who were unprepared were aware. This has a claim, an excellent claim, to be accepted as a historical representation of the teaching of Jesus; the occurrence in such a context of the saying about the Kingdom of God appearing in the midst is a strong reason for regarding it as genuine and tells us its historical interpretation. On the other hand, the Oxyrhynchus document gives us only an application of our Lord's words to changed conditions of time and place.

II

THE SYNOPTIC PROBLEM

WHEN we study the Gospels together, it is at once obvious that the Fourth Gospel, the Gospel according to John, stands apart from the others. For the most part the narratives and discourses which it contains are not found in the other three Gospels, while the matter contained in these is not found in the fourth. But the three Gospels of Matthew, Mark, and Luke have much in common. It is possible to arrange them in parallel columns, so that their common matter may be studied and compared at a glance. This was first done in a systematic way about a hundred years ago by J. J. Griesbach, who called this arrangement in parallel columns a Synopsis. From the time of Griesbach the Gospels of Matthew, Mark, and Luke have been called the Synoptic Gospels, and the problem of the relation of Matthew, Mark, and Luke to one another is the Synoptic Problem.

A century of investigation has brought the Gospel according to Mark into a generally acknowledged position of priority as a historical source. This has been effected almost entirely by internal considerations, by examining the common matter of Matthew, Mark, and Luke, comparing the parallel narratives as wholes and in detail, and by estimating the nature and significance of the peculiar characteristics of each of the three. External evidence, the testimony of ancient writers, is so scanty and obscure that little of direct value can be extracted from it. By about 180 A. D. we find our four Gospels already received in the church as a sacred and exclusive collection. This collection seems to have been already formed by the middle of the second century. Before that the several Gospels must have circulated independently. The Third Gospel, in fact, was designed by the writer of it to be the first volume of a longer historical work, of which our Acts of the Apostles forms the second. The Second Gospel is mutilated at the end; its text, according to the oldest manuscripts in Greek and the oldest Syriac version, ends at xvi. 8, in the middle of a sentence. This mutilation must have been accidental, for any intentional curtailment would have been made at a more suitable point: even xvi. 7 would have made a better finish. Therefore we may go on to infer that all our copies of the Gospel according to Mark are descended from a single copy, imperfect at the end and perhaps tattered elsewhere. As a matter of fact, there are one or two places in Mark, e. g. incomprehensible proper names like *Boanerges* and *Dalmanutha*, where the transmitted text can best be explained as the result of imperfect attempts to copy an illegible exemplar. But such places are few. On the whole, the text is satisfactory in essentials ; apart from the minor stylistic and harmonistic changes of scribes, we seem to have the work very much as it left the author's hand.

"Mark was known to the two other synoptic writers, when it was already in the same condition as we now have it, both in text and contents." So writes Wellhausen.[1] This is the result of the critical study of the Synoptic Gospels during the nineteenth century. Now that this result has been attained, it is easy to verify in its main outlines by any one who will compare for himself the common matter of Matthew, Mark, and Luke. It is possible to explain all, or almost all, the features of the Gospel narrative as we read it in Matthew and Luke on the supposition that it is based

[1] *Einleitung in die drei ersten Evangelien*, § 6, p. 57.

upon Mark, impossible to explain Mark on the supposition that it is based on a document similar to Matthew or Luke. The common order of the anecdotes is Mark's order; where Matthew deserts Mark's order, Mark is supported by Luke, where Luke deserts Mark's order, Mark is supported by Matthew. Matthew and Luke never agree in order against Mark. It is practically the same with the text itself as with the order of the narratives: Mark and Luke agree against Matthew, Matthew and Mark agree against Luke, while the points in which Matthew and Luke agree against Mark are so few and so insignificant in character that it seems unnecessary to postulate the existence of an earlier form of Mark — what used to be called in Germany *Ur-Marcus*, i. e. original Mark — in order to account for them.[1]

[1] See the discussion in the present writer's *Gospel History and its Transmission*, pp. 42–58, and also Sir John Hawkins' *Horae Synopticae*, 172 ff. (2d ed., 208 ff.).

But the demonstration of the relative priority of the Gospel according to Mark is only the first step in the criticism of the Synoptic Gospels. Mark may be older than Matthew or Luke, and may constitute one of the sources from which they were compiled. We must go on to consider the Gospel of Mark in itself as a historical document, and also to investigate the source and character of those large portions of Matthew and Luke that have no parallel in Mark, or at least cannot have been taken directly from Mark. We may admit that Matthew and Luke used Mark practically in the form which still survives, but was that the original form? Is the Gospel of Mark itself perhaps based on an earlier document? And can we trace in Matthew and Luke the use of any other document besides Mark?

It will be convenient to say a few words about the last question at this point. The

Gospels of Matthew and Luke mainly differ from that of Mark in that they contain a large number of sayings of Jesus not given by Mark. Many of these sayings are peculiar to Matthew or peculiar to Luke, but others are given in both, and often with such coincidences of language and of order that they must have been derived from a common source. Thus, for instance, Matthew v.–vii. (the so-called "Sermon on the Mount") is parallel to Luke vi. 20–49, and Matthew xi. 2–19 is practically repeated in Luke vii. 18–35. A comparison of these passages leads us to infer that Matthew and Luke have made use of a common source, written in Greek, which must have contained, amongst other things, sayings of Jesus about John the Baptist, together with a collection of ethical sayings which began with the Beatitudes and ended with the similitude of the houses built on the rock or on the river-bed. The common source, now lost, except so far as it is preserved in Matthew and Luke, it was formerly the fashion to call the "Logia," from a belief that it was mentioned under that name by Papias of Hierapolis in Asia Minor about the middle of the second century.[1] Wellhausen and others, however, call it "Q," i. e. *Quelle* (source), and this name is preferable, as we know so little of its origin or extent.

The common matter of Matthew and Luke, not shared by Mark, almost all consists of sayings of Jesus. We therefore assume that Q mainly consisted of sayings. But the same arguments that prove Q to have contained the "Sermon on the

[1] Papias (quoted by Eusebius, *Ch. History*, iii. 39) says: "Matthew indeed in the Hebrew language wrote down the *Logia*, and each interpreted them as he was able." What the work was to which Papias alludes is very doubtful: it is certain that our Gospel according to Matthew is a Greek work, based upon Greek sources, one of them being in fact our Gospel according to Mark.

Mount," or at least an earlier form of that collection of sayings, also prove Q to have contained the story of the healing of the centurion's boy. It is because Matthew (v. 3–vii. 27) and Luke (vi. 20–49) each contains a collection of sayings, beginning with beatitudes and ending with the similitude of the House on the Rock, that we infer a similar collection to have existed in Q. But this collection is followed, both in Matthew (viii. 3–13) and in Luke (vii. 1–10), by the story of the centurion. If our first inference be valid, then the story of the centurion must also be assigned to Q. Q therefore was not a mere assembly of sayings of Jesus, but also contained anecdotes about his wonderful works.

But when we have said this, we have said nearly everything that is absolutely certain. Professor Harnack in his book, "Sayings and Discourses of Jesus,"[1] has

[1] Harnack, *Sprüche und Reden Jesu*, 1907.

attempted to reconstruct Q from the sections of Matthew and Luke which he considers to have been derived from this lost document. But it is very doubtful whether his reconstruction can be accepted as anything more than a mass of genuine but detached fragments, and what we want is a picture of Q as a whole. We may agree that the sayings and discourses which Harnack assigns to Q really did form part of it, but we have very little reason to think that Q did not contain a great deal more.

One thing at least is clear. We can see by a comparison of Matthew and Luke with Mark that Matthew and Luke have used Mark, making it in fact the basis upon which their own Gospels have been planned. Between them they have managed to incorporate almost all the Gospel of Mark, and by comparing their works with the original, we can see pretty well the reasons which led them to drop or to modify those portions of Mark which they have severally dropped or modified. But we are able to see all this, because the Gospel of Mark is actually before us. If the Gospel of Mark were unknown to us, if its contents had to be inferred from Matthew and Luke, should we be able to reconstruct it at all? I do not think so. Even if by divination, rather than by legitimate criticism, we recognised as Marcan those sections which are retained only by Matthew or only by Luke, we should still miss all the vivid peculiarities of Mark. And when we are trying to estimate the tendencies and characteristics of the Gospel of Mark, it is just by the peculiarities of the work that its characteristics are revealed. If we were reconstructing Mark by the same process and with the same materials that we use for reconstructing Q, that is to say, by picking out the Marcan elements from Matthew and Luke, we should not arrive at a document in which our Lord says, "The Sabbath was made for man, and not man for the Sabbath," or one that tells us how his friends once thought he was mad, for these things are preserved neither by Matthew nor by Luke. We should not have any idea that the real Mark contained the parable of the ear of corn growing of itself. We should not know that it contained the Aramaic sayings, *Talitha cumi*, and *Ephphatha*, sayings which carry us back to the soil of Palestine. We could not have reconstructed out of Matthew and Luke the important historical notice that Jesus when he for the last time passed through Galilee "would not that any man should know it," or that he began his answer about the great commandment with the "Hear, O Israel!" All these things are features really characteristic of Mark; it is the presence of strongly individual features such as these in the Gospel of Mark that gives it its preëminence as a historical document. But not one of them would be found in a Mark reconstructed out of Matthew and Luke, and I cannot believe that our reconstructions of Q are any more like the real Q than our reconstructions of Mark would be like the real Mark.[1]

Another point also has to be taken into consideration. If the Gospel of Mark were not extant, and we had to infer its scope and contents from the Gospels of Matthew and Luke alone, is it not almost inevitable that we should have assigned to Mark some things that we now know to belong not to Mark but to Q? We do not know for certain that Matthew and Luke used only one common source besides Mark, and it remains possible that the mass of material which we regard as belonging to Q may

[1] See Harnack's *Sprüche und Reden Jesu* (1907), and the present writer's review of it in the *Journal of Theological Studies*, viii. 454–459.

have been drawn from at least two separate sources. It is conceivable, for instance, that the sayings of Jesus which relate to John the Baptist, together with the account of the Baptist's preaching, may have been derived from a document different from that which supplied the outline of the "Sermon on the Mount" and the Parables. I do not think it on the whole probable, but there is something to be said for it, and it is a possibility to be borne in mind.

What, then, it may be asked, do we gain by the recognition of this lost source Q, if we cannot reconstruct it? The answer, I believe, is this: that by recognising certain sayings in Matthew and Luke to have been drawn from the same source, we are better able to isolate the features in the sayings that are due to the several Evangelists, and thereby better able to understand what they meant in their original form. We cannot do without either the Lucan or the Matthæan form of the sayings, but we can use the one to control the other.

In any case, the material comprehended under the sign Q includes very many of the most precious jewels of the Gospel. When Justin Martyr in the second century wished to exhibit to the heathen Emperor the characteristic ethical teaching of Christ, nine tenths of his examples came out of passages derived from Q.[1] It is from Q that we have the blessing on the poor, the hungry, the reviled; from Q come "Love your enemies," "Turn the other cheek," "Be like your Father who maketh His sun to shine on the evil and the good," "Consider the lilies," "Be not anxious — your Father knoweth ye have need," "They shall come from east and west and sit down with Abraham in the kingdom of God." It is Q that tells us that the adversaries of Jesus found him not ascetic enough and

[1] Justin Martyr, *Apology*, i. 15 f.

mocked at him as a friend of tax-gatherers and sinners. It is Q that tells us that Jesus said "I thank thee, Father, that thou hast hidden these things from the wise and revealed them to babes,—even so, Father, for so it was pleasing in thy sight." If the work of Mark be more important to the historian, it is Q that supplies starting-points for the Christian moralist. Most important of all, it gives light and shade to the somewhat austere lines of the portrait of Jesus sketched in the Gospel of Mark.

The interest of Q is extremely great. It is great from what we actually know of it, and it possesses the fascination of the elusive and the unknown. It is well therefore to keep steadily in mind how little we can be certain even of the general plan of the work, or of what it did *not* contain. True it is that, as Justin says, "short and concise came words from Christ, for he was no sophist, but his word was a mighty work of God":

detached as the fragments of Q must remain to us, often devoid of context or presupposing totally different social conditions from those of our own age, yet the single sayings have again and again proved themselves instinct with truly divine power. Yet though they are jewels, they are for the most part jewels detached from their original setting, and this setting we cannot reconstruct as a whole. I am persuaded that Q is to us, and must remain, a collection of disconnected fragments.

III

THE GOSPEL ACCORDING TO MARK

THE question most in debate at present in the criticism of the Gospel history is whether the Gospel according to Mark gives us a generally faithful representation of the ministry of Jesus. On grounds mainly of literary criticism it is acknowledged that our Mark was used as a basis by the other synoptists. The Gospel of Mark is therefore more primitive as a whole than the Gospels of Matthew and Luke as wholes. But is Mark to be regarded as absolutely primitive? And even if we regard the analysis of Mark into its component factors as for us an insoluble problem, even if we regard all theories of an *Ur-Marcus* as baseless guesses, still there remains the inevitable question of the value of our Gospel of Mark as a historical source. At best it is a mere sketch of the career of Jesus Christ: but is it, we must ask, a trustworthy sketch?

The answer given by modern investigators to this most important question depends in the last resort upon the view that each one forms of the real work undertaken and accomplished by Jesus of Nazareth. Undoubtedly there are many, coming from very different philosophical and theological camps, to whom the Gospel according to Mark appears to be an inadequate interpretation of our Lord. It does not satisfy the modern philosophical liberal, who would like to regard the mission of Jesus as "purely religio-ethical and humanitarian."[1] The philosophical liberal finds fewer moral maxims in Mark than in Matthew and Luke, while at the same time he is shocked by the description of a number of miracles,

[1] B. W. Bacon, *Beginnings of Gospel Story*, p. xxxviii.

— mostly, it is true, of healing,— the details of which he feels himself obliged to explain away. But the picture drawn in Mark is hardly more satisfactory from the orthodox conservative point of view. In Wellhausen's phrase, "we hear of Disciples and we wonder how He comes to have them."[1] Till our eyes become accustomed to the atmosphere it is difficult to recognize the conventional Saviour, with the gentle unindividualized face, in the stormy and mysterious Personage portrayed by the second Gospel. "And they were in the way, going up to Jerusalem, and Jesus was going before them, and they were amazed, and some as they followed were afraid"[2] — as we read the story in Mark we follow Jesus on his way, and we hardly know why or whither. At least, we hardly know what is being told us, if we listen with modern presuppositions, instead of coming with

[1] *Einleitung*, p. 51. [2] Mark x. 32.

our minds full of the Jewish expectations of the Kingdom of God, as they took shape during the turbulent two centuries that preceded the crucifixion of Jesus.

The ultimate difficulty felt by so many modern critics about the Gospel of Mark is not the minor discrepancies in the narrative, though they are present, or the tales of miracle, for it is always possible to allow for unscientific description or exaggeration. The difficulty lies in its presentation of the actual contents of the "Gospel" itself and of the career of Jesus. According to these critics, Mark has not only put in features of the Ministry that he might have left out, he has left out things, and those the most important, that he ought to have put in. Where, they say, is the Teaching of Jesus? Mark gives us neither the Sermon on the Mount nor the Parable of the Prodigal Son. One who considers that Mark used Q confesses that the use made of it is "by no means characterized by sympathetic and appreciative insight."[1] And if, as tradition seems to assert, the ultimate source of the Evangelist's information be St. Peter himself, is it possible to suppose that the real characteristics of our Lord's career could have been thrown so completely out of focus?

It may readily be granted that most of these objections are weighty, if only we can be sure of the foundation upon which they rest. But it is the foundation itself that is insecure. The objections all assume that Jesus was really and primarily an ethical teacher, or a social reformer, or both. Now, if we regard Jesus from this point of view, it is true that many features in the Gospel of Mark can hardly be treated as historically accurate. The very ground plan

[1] Bacon, *Beginnings*, p. xx. That such a judgment has to be passed upon Mark's use of Q is an argument for disbelieving that Mark knew Q at all.

of the work becomes incredible. It becomes impossible to comprehend or to justify the journey of Jesus to Jerusalem, or to obtain an intelligible picture of his doings and sayings when he arrived there. Both from the liberals and from the conservatives we hear that the Paschal week is too short a period for "the Jerusalem ministry." If the object of Jesus in going to Jerusalem was to teach there, then the time allowed by Mark is insufficient. If his object were "a program of peaceful reform in the interest of the masses,"[1] we can only say that it was eminently unsuccessful. And if his object in going to Jerusalem was, as Mark seems to tell us, simply to be killed, is not that irrational, the act of a fanatic? Was it worthy of the founder of the religion of the civilized world?

It is perhaps not out of place to remind ourselves that this is not the first time the

[1] Bacon, *Beginnings*, p. 158.

Way of the Cross has been accounted foolishness both by philosophers and by traditionalists; for the doctrine set forth by Mark is the Doctrine of the Cross. To such an extent is this the case that the Evangelist is commonly supposed in critical theories to have derived his conception of Christ's work from St. Paul. To quote Professor Bacon once more: "The Paulinism of Mark is supremely manifest in this evangelist's whole conception of what constitutes the apostolic message"; it is "the continual reiteration of the doctrine, 'He that would save his life shall lose it.'"[1] Of course this is Paulinism; but what if Paulinism in this respect was really "the mind of Christ"?

Once more it may be well to point out the very peculiar position occupied by the Gospel of Mark in the history of early Christian literature, for it is this peculiar

[1] *Beginnings*, pp. xxvii, xxviii.

position that compels us to weigh with the utmost care and deference the story that it offers to us. On the one hand there is nothing in Christian literature to indicate that the Gospel of Mark was ever popular or official, or that it was written to suit the taste of any community that has left any trace in history. Irenaeus says somewhere that Mark was used by the Docetic heretics; but he brings forward no evidence in support of his statement, which seems a mere theory made to correspond with the use of Luke by the Marcionites and of Matthew by the Ebionites. If existing evidence be any reflex of actual use, the Gospel of Mark was, and has been till the present day, unpopular and neglected. It is, in fact, more or less of a puzzle how it came to be included in the Church's Canon. It is written in an uncultivated style, and it occupies itself with those parts and aspects of the Gospel story concerning which Greek-speaking Christians seem to have taken very little interest, until the rise of the cult of the Holy Places in Palestine toward the very end of the second century A. D. I find it difficult to believe that a book of this kind is the work of an eclectic, who combined Pauline doctrine with Petrine traditions and wove them together into a strange and rough, yet vigorous tale. Moreover — and this is the discovery of modern literary criticism — this unpopular Gospel was indeed used by one class of persons, *viz.* those who after Mark attempted to tell the story of Jesus Christ. St. Luke informs us in his preface that "many," before he himself wrote, had taken in hand to draw up some account of Christian origins; but however many there may have been, he uses the Gospel of Mark for one of the main sources of his own work. The Gospel according to Matthew to a still greater degree is based upon Mark. It seems almost as if these writers had been compelled to use a writing which no one else cared to quote.

Surely the natural inference to be drawn is that the point of view from which Mark had written was already antiquated when the later synoptic Evangelists made their compilations. The Gospel of Mark may perhaps be the work of a less cultivated mind than that of the other Gospel writers; at any rate it comes before us as a document belonging to an earlier stage in the development of Christian ideas than the other Gospels. If then we find it animated by ideas which do occur in Paul, though during the second century they find hardly any echo in orthodox Christian literature, some part of the resemblance may be due to its primitive age and character. In any case, it is our plain duty to weigh well the story told in this venerable document, before we reject it in favour of modern reconstructions of the course of events.

Naturally we need not expect any impossible standard of accuracy or insight. The question at issue is not of the presentation of details, but of the general view. It is not claimed that the second Evangelist was by nature or by training a specially gifted historian, but he was too much in touch with the events to give a wholly distorted account of them. The writer of the Fourth Gospel may perhaps have a claim to be heard as an interpreter of Jesus Christ: the office of Mark is rather to be a witness of what men saw and heard.

The Kingdom of God and the "Son of Man."

What, then, is the general conception of the mission of Jesus set before us in the Gospel of Mark? We may begin with two or three quotations from Professor Bacon, who is all the better witness as he is a convinced opponent of apocalyptic eschatology.

He speaks of "the sane and well-poised mind of the plain mechanic of Nazareth," and regards the apocalyptic elements in the Gospels as later additions made by "the enthusiastic Church."[1] Yet even Professor Bacon says, and says most justly: "For some reason Jesus *did* go up to Jerusalem, and throw down the gauntlet in the face of the priestly hierocracy in the temple itself. For some reason he *did* follow a rôle that led to his execution by Pilate as a *political* agitator. For some reason his followers, very shortly after, *did* ascribe to him not mere reappearance from the tomb, but exaltation to the place of the Messiah 'at the right hand of God'—attributes so exalted that it is difficult to believe they had no other foundation than mere reverence for an admired Teacher."[2] And again (on Mark ix. 1): "We cannot do honest justice to the unbroken consensus

[1] Bacon, *Beginnings*, p. 108. [2] *Beginnings*, p. 106.

of primitive testimony without acknowledging that Jesus pointed his disciples to the expected intervention of God, which should be the vindication of his gospel, before the generation which heard and rejected it should have passed away."[1] This is well and justly said; but does it not show that formulas like "the sane and well-poised mind of the plain mechanic of Nazareth" are inadequate, if not altogether inappropriate, as a characterization of Jesus? If we rationalize overmuch the ideas and the hopes of Jesus and his friends, how are we to account for their invincible enthusiasm?

"The vindication of his gospel"—but what was the Gospel of Jesus? According to Mark it consisted in the announcement that the Kingdom of God was at hand.[2] Everything else was inference and deduction from this fundamental idea.

[1] *Beginnings*, p. 120. [2] Mark i. 15.

The Kingdom of God is indeed familiar to us as a religious phrase, but the conception itself is strange, because at this period of the world's history no one but the socialists are expecting a great change, and that a change for the better, in the conditions of human life. It was otherwise with the Jewish nation in the first century of our era. For two hundred years, ever since the martyrs in the days before the Maccabees, the martyrs who had preferred to die rather than give up the customs of their inherited religion, the struggle between Judaism and civilization had gone on. The military successes of Judas Maccabaeus and his family secured to all the Jews the undisturbed exercise of their religion, and the outward history of Palestine degenerated into an entirely secular and somewhat sordid game of politics, with the irresistible might of Rome looming ever more insistently in the background. But this was only one side of the great duel. It was a war of ideas, a war between civilization and religion, in the modern sense of these terms. On the side of the Gentiles was philosophy, science, art, good government, all the material goods of this life; on the side of the Jew was the ineradicable conviction that the Lord and Maker of all things visible and invisible had chosen Israel and taught it the way of Life and Death, and that in comparison with this all other privileges and advantages were as nothing. Judaism was a conscious rival to civilization, as civilization was then understood. That the 'Gentiles' were aware of this we can see from the references to the Jews in contemporary classical literature, where they are represented as a strange unnatural race, distinct from other human beings.

Such a condition of things does not endure for long. An isolated race cannot permanently maintain its ideals in the face of the civilized world. In the political sphere the end came in A. D. 70, when, the Jews having at last broken out into open rebellion against the Gentile yoke, the Jewish State was destroyed and the Temple worship abolished. The Judaism that survived, and survives to this day, is really rather a posthumous child of the older Judaism than the older Judaism itself. It is rather to be regarded as the younger sister of Christianity than its mother. The older Judaism perished, but its children survived.

During the long struggle with the world outside, the hopes of the Jews expressed themselves in forms very different from what actually came to pass. These hopes find expression in the long series of apocalyptic books that appeared at intervals throughout the whole period, from the Book of Daniel in 168 B. C., just before the Maccabaean rising, to the Apocalypse of

Baruch, written after the Destruction of Jerusalem by Titus; and it is from these books we can trace the rise and development of that belief in the coming Kingdom of God which is assumed in the New Testament. The books are now, with the exception of the Book of Daniel, rejected both by the Rabbinical Jews and by nearly all Christian bodies, for when the New Age came, the imperfect forecasts of it lost their interest Rabbinical Judaism rejected the hopes which belonged to a time when the Jews were still a nation, and the Christian Church gradually came to do the same, although the Church was in a special sense the heir of the Apocalyptists.

The main idea of the Kingdom of God is found already in the Book of Daniel. The fundamental notion is that the Most High is indeed Autocrat, He alone has sovereignty, but He hands it over for a time and for His own inscrutable purposes to whomsoever He will.[1] At any given moment there is a world-power, the Babylonian, the "Median," the Persian, the Seleucid Greek. But this will not be for ever. In the end the Most High Himself will take the dominion into His own hands. The Kingdom of God Himself will be inaugurated, and He will reign for ever, protecting His faithful people and rewarding them for all the trials they have undergone at the hands of the heathen.

This is the apocalyptic hope. It is the correlative of the conflict between Jewish religion and the Græco-Roman civilization. To do it justice, we must remember that this conflict to the Jews was one between religious faith and material civilization: if the Kingdom of God were to come at all, it would come not by material weapons but by the operation of God. Material force was on the other side. And so the Christian

[1] Daniel iv. 17.

is taught to pray "Thy Kingdom come," because it is for God, not for man, to bring it in. When the time is ripe, it will come.

The Christ or Messiah, that is, the Anointed of God, is one of the features of the coming Kingdom. His function is to judge the heathen and to rule as God's Vicegerent over the Saints, when the Great Day arrives. The Christ does not bring in the Kingdom,—that is the work of God Himself; the Christ only enters on his office when all is ready. He is, in fact, one of the personages of the New Age, not the person through whom the New Age is brought in. If he be conceived of as existing beforehand, then he is not yet properly the Christ. It is most important to keep this in mind when we read the Gospels, as otherwise the command of Jesus that Peter should be silent about his Messiahship becomes incomprehensible. Before the time Jesus may be Messiah in God's sight, to whom to think is to do.[1] He may be Messiah to the demons, but to men He is not yet Messiah. It was for God to make Him manifest, not for men.

Was there then any Scripture that had spoken of the Messiah before he became Messiah? And if so, by what title had he been spoken of? The answer is, that he was the Man from Heaven spoken of by Enoch.

Here we come to the closely allied questions of the influence of the Book of Enoch upon primitive Christianity, and of the meaning of the title "Son of Man." The Son of Man—as curious a phrase in Greek as in English—is a literal translation of the Aramaic for "the human being," "the Man." It is evident that no one could take "the Man" as a title for himself or his office without something further being understood. If any one calls himself "the Man,"

[1] Enoch xiv. 22.

it must mean "the Man — you know who." When therefore Jesus speaks of himself as "the Son of Man," a phrase in Aramaic identical with "the Man," he must mean "the Man — you know whom I speak of." And when we notice that this Man is one who "comes with the clouds of heaven," with whom is associated functions of judgment at the great Assize, it is clear that the Man who is meant is the celestial Man of Daniel vii. 13, a symbolical figure that stands for the Kingdom of the Saints, in contrast to the bestial figures that come up from the sea, which symbolize the heathen empires.

In Daniel the Man is not individualized. He stands for the nation, not for the Messiah. But in the Similitudes of Enoch, the figure of Daniel, the Son of Man who was with the Ancient of Days,[1] is personified and individualized. From of old this Son

[1] Enoch xlvi. 2.

of Man, this celestial human being, has been hidden with the Most High,[1] but one day he will be revealed. The kings and the mighty, i.e., the heathen rulers of the world, will see and be terrified and beg for mercy in vain. The angels will drag them away to punishment, but the righteous will be saved and protected, and with that Son of Man they will rejoice for ever and ever.[2]

The Book of Enoch is a strange barbarous work, without poetry, without charm. It has long been rejected from the Bible by every branch of the Church save the barbarian Christians of Abyssinia. Are we, it may be asked, really to seek the origin of the title of our Lord, round which so many pathetic associations have grown, in this fierce and narrow Jewish apocalypse? And if this was the hope of the Gospel, was it justified? In what sense can it be said that the Kingdom of God was at hand?

[1] Enoch xlviii. 3–7. [2] Enoch lxii. 11, 14.

These are fundamental questions for our estimate of Christianity, but they are equally fundamental for the criticism and exegesis of the Gospels. To those who have learned to see the vital principle of the Christian movement in this expectation of the supernatural Kingdom of God, sentence after sentence of the Gospels, saying after saying, parable after parable, falls into its place. And in no document is this clearer than in the Gospel of Mark. The answer we give to the second question will depend almost entirely upon our personal attitude to the Church, to the Christian movement as a whole. Christianity *is* Judaism recreated in a form that could thrive in, and finally absorb, the civilization of Europe: if Christianity be of God, then the Kingdom of God did come to men. It is the new dispensation of the Christian Church; "the new race of Christians"[1] are the citizens of the

[1] The phrase is used, e. g., by Bardesanes.

Kingdom of God. And Jesus Christ is, as Tacitus had rightly heard, "the originator of that name"; not that he was the originator of the idea of the Kingdom of God, or that he was the teacher of the Christians, but because he was and remained the source of their inspiration. His words in part, but still more his life and death, kindled the fire of the Christian movement.

As for the Book of Enoch, the evidence does point very strongly to the great influence it exercised on primitive Christianity. The date of Enoch is a matter of dispute, and the accepted theory is that it is made up of several parts, of different dates. But it is certainly Palestinian, and it existed in its present form at the beginning of the Christian era. It is quoted by name in the Epistle of Jude, a letter that used to be dated much later than necessary, as long as apocalyptic ideas were out of fashion. It is certainly referred to in the First Epistle of Peter, whatever the date of that work may be; and it was long held in honour among the Christians, who took it for a genuine prophecy of Enoch, "the seventh from Adam." But it is especially in the Gospels that we see its influence, in Q as much as in Mark. The theory of demons and demoniacal possession, implied in Luke xi. 24–26 (Matthew xii. 43–45), a passage certainly drawn from Q, is exactly that set forth at length in Enoch; and the judgment scene in Matthew xxv. 31 ff ("the Sheep and the Goats") loses half its meaning, if the corresponding scene in Enoch lxii, where "the Son of Man" is shewn "sitting on the throne of his glory," be not presupposed. Enoch is crude and fierce, the corresponding words of the Gospel are instinct with spiritual power. Yes; but "that is not first which is spiritual, but that which is natural, afterwards that which is spiritual."

The Gospel of Mark tells us how Jesus of Nazareth came announcing the impending advent of the Kingdom of God and bidding those who heard to repent and prepare themselves. The population of Galilee are generally friendly, but then as always the number of those who are whole-hearted is few: the people as a whole do not repent.[1] And, to adopt the imagery of Jesus' own parable of the Ear of Corn,[2] if the fruit be not ripe, how can it be expected that the Lord of the Harvest will put the sickle to the corn? How can it be expected that God will bring in the New Age, if the people be not ready? Jesus is conscious that he is the destined Messiah, but the time for his manifestation is not yet. To acclaim him as Messiah before the Kingdom of God comes is premature.[3] Meanwhile, Jesus has

[1] Mark viii. 12, 38; ix, 19.
[2] Mark iv. 26–29.
[3] Mark viii. 29, 30.

another work before him. He will go up to Jerusalem.

It is evident from all the Gospel accounts that the adherents of the Galilean Prophet expected something great from the journey to Jerusalem. But Jesus knows that he is setting out on a forlorn hope, and will have no one to follow after him who is not prepared to give up everything "for the Gospel."[1] What his own thoughts about this momentous expedition were may best be gathered from the Parable of the Wicked Husbandmen.[2] Perhaps, after all, the nation and its rulers would reverence the Son of the Lord of the Vineyard, and would give at his summons the fruit of devotion and repentance. But it is clear that that was not the result that Jesus anticipated.

[1] Mark viii. 34–36; x. 21 ff.

[2] Mark xii. 1–11. See Burkitt, *The Parable of the Wicked Husbandmen*, in the Proceedings of the Third Congress of Religions, Oxford, 1908, vol. ii, 321–328.

Unless our Gospels embody a wholly distorted tradition, Jesus expected to die a violent death at the hands of the rulers of Jerusalem. His whole course of action was that of one who desires to precipitate a crisis which he believes to be inevitable. He did not announce himself as Messiah, yet he acted as if he were armed with complete authority. He refused to allow his actions to be supported by force; God would justify him in due time. There was an hour in Gethsemane when he shrank from the ordeal; there was a moment on the cross when he despaired. But with these exceptions he carried through the part of the Son of the Lord of the Vineyard without flinching to the end.

The end of the Gospel of Mark is mutilated; the narrative breaks off suddenly at xvi. 8, in the midst of the alarm and amazement of the women at the rock-cut tomb, who cannot find the body of Jesus. Had the true conclusion been preserved, no doubt we should have read of that appearance of the risen Lord to Peter,[1] which seems to have been psychologically the decisive rallying-point of the scattered and disheartened disciples. As we know, the new movement did not come to an end with the crucifixion. The Kingdom of God was soon to be made manifest (so the little band that rallied round Peter continued to believe), for their Master was not dead but had been raised to heaven, to sit at God's right hand, till the Kingdom came at last, when Jesus of Nazareth who had been crucified would appear as Christ, as the Son of Man spoken of by Daniel, to judge the quick and the dead.

Perhaps it was a dream, but at least it was a dream that captured the ancient world, and, as Professor Bacon says, in a

[1] 1 Cor. xv. 5: cf. Mark xvi. 7.

phrase already quoted, "mere reverence for an admired Teacher" is not sufficient to account for the hopes and the claims of the Christians. And therefore the Gospel of Mark, which makes so much of transcendental hopes and claims, which bases so much on the personal ascendency of Jesus, is more likely to reflect the historical truth than any view which regards the mission of Jesus as "purely religio-ethical and humanitarian."[1]

Considerations of the kind put forward in this chapter appeal with different force to different minds, and it must be acknowledged that many students of early Christianity still hesitate to accept the tale of the public career of Jesus as told in the Gospel of Mark, though it be the oldest source we possess. There are those who try to read between the lines, who think

[1] Bacon, *Beginnings*, p. xxxviii.

that behind the cross-bars of Jewish eschatology and Pauline theologizing they can discern a gracious, if shadowy figure, giving utterance to "ethical ideas that are the essential element in the spiritual experience of the modern world."[1] Professor Peabody, from whom I quote, goes on to say: "There is nothing apocalyptic in the parable of the Good Samaritan, or in the appropriation by Jesus of the two great commandments, or in the prayer for to-day's bread and the forgiveness of trespasses, or in the praise of peace-making and purity of heart. Yet in these, and not in the mysterious prophecies of an approaching desolation, the conscience of the world has found its Counsellor and Guide."[2] Those who put the centre of gravity of our Lord's work in the enunciation of sayings such as

[1] Professor W. Herrmann, quoted by F. G. Peabody, *Transactions of the Oxford Congress of Religions*, ii, 308.

[2] *Ibid.*, p. 309.

these are undoubtedly dissatisfied with the proportions of the portrait sketched in the Gospel of Mark.

A detailed reply might be made to arguments like Professor Peabody's. Indeed, the apocalyptic background behind much of our Lord's ethical teaching, notably that about "daily bread," can, I think, actually be recognized. But however this may be, for the student of history the first necessity is not to lay emphasis upon those parts of the remembered words of Jesus which happen to strike an immediate chord in our ethical consciousness. The first necessity is to place him in due relation to the strange and far-off time in which he lived among men. The first thing we have to account for is the enthusiasm and the devotion of those who claimed to be his followers and apostles. "Let the children first be filled"; we must first of all think of our Lord in connexion with the aspirations of his own time and his own country, and be ourselves content with the crumbs that have fallen down into our very different world. After all, the table was spread for the lost sheep of the House of Israel, not for us.

In the end, a frank recognition that the Gospel as a whole looks forward to near and overwhelming catastrophe may be found not inconsistent with due reverence for the always wonderful sayings that light up the Gospel story. However we may look at it, the rise of Christianity is a wonderful, a most wonderful tale. It must always remain a portent to be marvelled at, a thing that cannot wholly be explained. And it is therefore not surprising that Jesus himself cannot wholly be explained. It is not likely that he can really be comprehended under a modern formula, whether ecclesiastical or unecclesiastical. And therefore it is not likely that we are getting any nearer to historical truth, when we desert the earliest ascertainable historical tradition about him, the tradition that is preserved for us in the Gospel according to Mark.

IV

POSSIBLE "SOURCES" OF THE GOSPEL OF MARK

TRADITION says that the Gospel of Mark embodies St. Mark's reminiscences of what he had heard St. Peter say. On the whole, this is doubted by modern critics; is it possible to obtain any plausible view on the subject? The preceding section was necessary, in order to meet the general objection that Mark gives a distorted view of the Ministry; but how does the case stand with regard to details? Christian tradition, we may remark, does not represent the number of original witnesses that were available as large. When St. Luke is describing the election of a thirteenth apostle to take the place of Judas Iscariot, he makes it plain that only two of the rallied band of

Disciples had "companied" with Peter and the rest from the beginning of the Ministry.

It may further be noted that the question of St. Mark's sources has been greatly modified by the progress made with the Synoptic problem. So long as our three Gospels according to Matthew, Mark, and Luke were believed to be so many specimens of a common Evangelical tradition, it seemed impossible to particularize the sources of individual features of the narrative. Tradition connected St. Peter with our Second Gospel, but there is little in it about St. Peter that is not shared by the others; so that it was difficult to understand what special part St. Peter could have had in it. But now conditions are changed. The Gospel of Mark is not simply more faithful than the others to the Synoptic norm: it was itself the originator of the Synoptic norm, the direct source of the "Synoptic" element in the others. It has become improbable that there was any common Evangelical tradition at all about the course of our Lord's Ministry. We no longer have to ask whether Mark has a better claim than Matthew or Luke to be regarded as the Gospel according to Peter; we have now to ask whether Mark has a better claim to this title than the document or documents grouped under the sign Q, or than the Gospel of John, or than the types now represented by various fragments from Oxyrhynchus. If, as seems likely, we have in the Gospel of Mark the tale of the Ministry of our Lord told for the first time as a connected whole from the Voice at the baptism till after his resurrection, what we have to ask is how far this narrative, this general scheme of the Ministry, is based upon what the Evangelist had gathered from Simon Peter. It may be as well to remind ourselves here that we do not know how far the narrative extended over the ground covered by St. Luke's Acts of the Apostles. The first half of that work ends with the name of John who was surnamed Mark, and it is plausible to suppose that it may have been in the work of Mark that our Third Evangelist came across the life-like episode of Rhoda.[1]

Two remarks of Wellhausen about the Gospel of Mark may here be recorded. "The tradition which Mark embodies is comparatively full about Jerusalem, meagre about Galilee";[2] i.e. the one Week in Jerusalem occupies more than a third of the whole narrative. And again: "The single scenes are often told in a life-like style without unessential additions and reflections, but they stand for the most part as a mere collection of disconnected anecdotes."[3] These facts, as Wellhausen shows, form a serious objection to regard-

[1] Acts xii. 13 ff. [2] Wellhausen, *Einleitung*, p. 52.
[3] *Einleitung*, p. 51.

ing Simon Peter, or any other Galilean, as the planner of the work; but I venture to think they are consistent with the authorship of "John who was surnamed Mark."

There is one incident in the Gospel of Mark which is absolutely pointless as it stands, namely, the incident of the youth who tried to follow Jesus after his arrest in the Garden; it is difficult to avoid the inference that the youth was the Evangelist himself, and that he is giving his personal experience. Can we doubt that it was he who saw and heard in Gethsemane, when Peter and James and John were sleeping? It may even be conjectured that the Last Supper itself was held in the house of Mary the mother of John Mark,[1] and that the dating by days, almost after the manner of a diary, which characterizes the story from Palm Sunday onwards, corresponds to actual reminiscences of the author, who had lived

[1] Cf. Acts xii. 12.

through the events of that memorable week when a boy, and had himself been a witness of some of them. This assumes that the final visit to Jerusalem did indeed only last a week, but I have endeavoured to show that the eschatological point of view, from which alone this short period is sufficient, is the true historical view.

For the rest of the Ministry the Evangelist must have been dependent on the information of others, and his narrative seems to me to be very much the kind of narrative that one in the position of John Mark might have been expected to compose. The earliest tradition — whatever it may be worth — does not represent Mark as writing in the lifetime of Peter. The first generation of Christians, as we have already seen, took little thought for preserving "the beginning of the Gospel of Jesus Christ," and there is nothing to show that the Evangelist had taken in hand to draw up an account of the Ministry until the Apostles, and with them the first-hand memory of eye-witnesses of our Lord's public career, had gone to their long home. The memory that still lived was that of the tales which the eye-witness used to tell: that is, striking scenes were remembered, memorable sayings, memorable anecdotes, rather than the sequence and proportion of the whole as it might have appeared to an outsider. The impression I get on reading the Gospel according to Mark is that many of the tales may be traditional, told perhaps again and again, and that some are already on the point of becoming conventionalized and epic, but that the sequence of them, the general scheme of the Ministry as a whole, is being constructed by the Evangelist for the first time. "Mark wrote down accurately, though not in order, all that he remembered"; is it not possible that the confused statement of Papias really implies no more than this, that no traditional sequence, no itinerary of our Lord's footsteps, was ever preserved by those who accompanied him?

Be this as it may, the Gospel of Mark, notwithstanding that it is the foundation for the other Synoptic Gospels, gives us only a disjointed narrative. Up to viii. 27 it is not much more than a collection of anecdotes. At viii. 27 begins the journey to Jerusalem from the north: from that point we need not doubt that Mark presents a chronological series of events, though even here there are gaps about which little is said. But all that goes before might more appropriately be called "scenes from the Ministry of Jesus" than an account of the Ministry. At the same time the scenes, speaking generally, appear to be arranged in their natural order: I see no reason for doubting that the revival in Galilee,[1] the

[1] Mark i. 14 f.

call of Simon with the first preaching at Capernaum,[1] the breach with the Pharisees,[2] the sending out of the twelve,[3] "the feeding of the five thousand" followed by wanderings out of Galilee,[4] the voyage to Bethsaida and on to Cæsarea Philippi,[5] represent the real sequence of events. Certainly nothing that is to be found in any other of the Gospels has any better claim to give the true sequence.

Minor inaccuracies of the Evangelist.

There are certain minor inaccuracies in the Gospel according to Mark that throw some light on the general standard of trustworthiness that he may be supposed to attain. In Mark ii. 26 he represents Jesus as saying that David entered into the House of God and ate the shewbread when Abiathar was high priest.[6] This is a mistake;

[1] Mark i. 16–39. [2] ii.–iii., culminating at iii. 6.
[3] vi. 7 ff. [4] vi. 30–vii. 31. [5] viii. 1–27.
[6] See Swete's note on the passage.

the event occurred in the lifetime of Abiathar, but the high priest was not Abiathar, but his father Ahimelech (or, as some authorities call him, Abimelech). The importance of the matter is that it shows the Evangelist to have had a certain measure of ignorance or carelessness, whether he were John Mark, or some one else. The clause is omitted by Matthew and Luke, presumably because of its inconsistency with the Book of Samuel, though doubtless it stood in the copy of Mark they severally used. We learn therefore that Mark is capable of perpetrating a historical blunder in a matter of "Jewish Antiquities," in regard to which he might well have been better informed.

It would not have been worth while to call attention to this well-known piece of inaccuracy, were it not that there are several others which appear to me to be of essentially the same nature, i. e. that they arise simply from carelessness and confusion in the writer.[1] As however certain of them seem to imply an inaccurate knowledge of Jewish customs rather than an inaccurate knowledge of the Old Testament, they have been held to indicate that the Evangelist had not himself been born a Jew. The first is the statement in Mark vii. 3 ff, that "the Pharisees and all the Jews" regularly practised certain ablutions, some of which (it is said) were practised only by those of priestly descent. Accepting this correction, we may surely regard the exaggeration in vii. 3 ff as merely a piece of carelessness, similar to that about Abiathar. If Mark was the cousin of Barnabas the Levite,[2] he may have confused ritual that he had seen practised in the home of his

[1] It may be noted here that, according to Josephus, the first husband of Herodias was not called Philip, as in Mark vi. 17, but Herod. The mistake is silently corrected in Luke iii. 19.

[2] Colossians iv. 10.

boyhood with the customs observed by all his fellow countrymen.

The other matter is more serious. The Second Evangelist is the chief authority for identifying the Last Supper with the paschal meal, an identification which seems to contradict all the other traditions about the date of the crucifixion, including that which served as the foundation for the narrative of the Second Gospel itself, and to be exceedingly improbable historically. Moreover, the Evangelist introduces this peculiar date by what is practically a contradiction in terms.[1] It is held by many scholars that no Jew could have perpetrated this statement, for the first day of the unleavened bread was the 15th of Nisan; but they used to sacrifice the passover on the 14th of Nisan.[2]

[1] Mark xiv. 12: "On the first day of the unleavened bread, when they used to sacrifice the passover."

[2] According to our reckoning these two events fell on the same civil day, for the Jewish day begins at sunset. The

The error is a very curious and important one, and I think that Professor Bacon is right in connecting it with the maintenance of the Roman practice of celebrating Easter always on a Sunday, and not, as the ancient churches of Asia Minor did, by the days of the Jewish month.[1] Be that as it may, the statement in Mark xiv. 12 after all only argues the same inattention to the Old Testament as that about Abiathar in Mark ii. 26, for the statements in Leviticus xxiii. 5, 6, about the dates of Passover and Unleavened Bread, are perfectly clear to every one that reads them, be he Jew or Gentile. Moreover, if you reckon by Roman (and English) days, the slaying of the paschal lambs and the eating of the paschal

first day of Unleavened Bread (Nisan 15) begins at sunset, the paschal lambs having been slain a few hours before on what we should call the *same* day, but which the Jews reckoned as the closing hours of Nisan 14.

[1] Bacon, *Beginnings of Gospel Story*, pp. xxix ff., 195–198.

should a narrative founded upon Peter's reminiscences show special regard for Peter? If there be any foundation for the tradition which connects the Gospel of Mark with the reminiscences of Simon Peter,—and apart from this connexion it is not easy to understand how this Gospel came to be preserved at all,—then we may expect to find in it features of the Ministry of Jesus that were really fixed in Peter's mind rather than adumbrations of "Petrine claims." Peter may never appear individually on the scene except for purposes of rebuke, as Professor Bacon remarks;[1] but is this feature of the narrative unlikely to have proceeded from Peter himself? All the Gospels tell the story of Peter's confession of Jesus as the Christ: it was indeed a historical moment of immense importance for the company of disciples. But is it psychologically unsuitable that the Gospel which tradition

[1] *Beginnings*, p. xxvii.

associates with the reminiscences of Simon Peter should also emphasize the rebuke which the Master administered to him almost at the moment of his confession?

Apart from this, the general character of the Gospel seems to me to harmonize well enough with the tradition that Mark's main source for his work was the tales he had heard from St. Peter. It is from the time of the "call" of Peter that the narrative first becomes particularized, and it is mainly round the Sea of Galilee that recorded incidents occur. Had the end of Mark been preserved, there can be little doubt, from the mention of Peter in xvi. 7, that we should have had a more detailed account of what Peter saw of his risen Lord than can be conjectured from Luke xxiv. 34 and 1 Corinthians xv. 5. The real objection raised against regarding St. Peter as the main authority for the stories told in the Second Gospel is that the resulting picture of Jesus Christ is inadequate or false. But I have attempted to show that, if we frankly accept the eschatological point of view, there is little difficulty in accepting the main outlines of the narrative as a not unfaithful picture of the general course of the Ministry.

Not all the tales in the second Gospel need be supposed to come direct from St. Peter or from the youthful reminiscences of the Evangelist. I have elsewhere[1] suggested that the tale of the Demoniac and the Swine[2] may have come to the Evangelist from Gerasa rather than direct from the companions of Jesus. Where and how the story of Herod and John the Baptist took shape it is impossible to say: Josephus[3] tells us that many people in Galilee regarded the defeat of Antipas by the Arabian King Aretas, his aggrieved father-in-law, as a

[1] *Journal of Biblical Literature*, xxvii. 132.

[2] Mark v. 20.

[3] *Antiquities*, xviii. 5, 2.

judgment upon him for his unlawful marriage with Herodias.

To sum up, the view of the Gospel according to Mark here advanced is that it is a work put together by one who seems to have been present as a youth at the arrest of Jesus in Gethsemane, but was not otherwise a companion of the Ministry. A generation later he formed the design of writing an account of the public career of the Lord, after almost all the witnesses had died, naturally or as martyrs. There is no valid reason to doubt that during some part of his adult life he had accompanied St. Peter, and that he has derived much of his material from what Peter had told him. But there is nothing to make us suppose that the general plan of the work comes from St. Peter, or that the first half of it should be regarded as more than a collection of anecdotes, arranged only in approximate chronological sequence. From the time of Peter's confession in the country of Cæsarea Philippi we get a real sequence of events, conditioned by the real nexus of the journey south to Jerusalem, though the sequence is not without gaps. For the week's stay in (or rather, near) Jerusalem at the Passover, we have a chronological scheme that may be accepted as historical, though it is disfigured by a serious inconsistency, whereby the Last Supper is reckoned as a Paschal Meal. This however was dictated by liturgical rather than historical reasons, and is contradicted by the rest of the narrative. It is assumed here that the Gospel is imperfect at the end, and it is regarded as not unlikely that it originally extended over much of the period covered by the first twelve chapters of the Acts of the Apostles.

V

THE COMPOSITION OF MATTHEW AND LUKE

THE reasons which lead the present writer to believe that we cannot, with any approach to certainty, reconstruct Q, the lost common source of Matthew and Luke, have been already given. Something may however be said of the methods which Matthew and Luke seem to have used in treating the material under their hand. From the way that they use the Gospel of Mark, which we actually possess, we may not unfairly conjecture how they treated their other sources, which we do not possess.

It is perhaps advisable to point out in the first place that both Matthew and Luke treat Mark with entire literary freedom. Mark meal with unleavened bread did take place on the same "day." The misdating of the Last Supper, whereby the Jewish Passover is turned into the first Christian Eucharist, is a more serious matter than a mere careless confusion between Jewish and Roman "days," but it is quite possible that the Easter Eucharistic Feast was already regarded in Rome as the Christian equivalent of the Jewish Passover meal when St. Mark wrote, and that he had to harmonize this view as best he could with the historical data that had been transmitted to him.

A word may be said here upon the character of the special references to St. Peter in the Gospel according to Mark. "Sight by hypnotic suggestion has few more curious illustrations than the discovery by writers under the spell of the Papias tradition of traces in Mark of special regard for Peter!" says Professor Bacon.[1] But why

[1] *Beginnings*, p. xxv.

is used by the other evangelists as valuable material; but they freely omit what seemed to them unsuitable or obscure, they add fresh material from other sources, working it into the Marcan narrative, each in accordance with his own literary methods, and they freely change the wording of the sayings and doings of Jesus. But while they are equally free in dealing with Mark, the manner in which they treat it is different. Matthew retains nearly all the material of Mark, and a plausible reason can be found for the omission of almost every verse that he does omit. But the matter from Mark is often welded together with matter from elsewhere, in such a way as to make it difficult to separate the two elements in detail.[1]

[1] E. g. Matt. iv. 11[b] doubtless comes from Mark i. 13[b]. The story of the Centurion (Matt. viii. 5–13) and that of the two would-be followers (viii. 19–22) are inserted in the middle of a whole set of anecdotes taken from Mark. Matt. xii. 22–32 is welded together from Mark iii. 20–30 and from the source of Luke xi. 14–23, xii. 10.

Luke, on the other hand, omits a good deal of Mark, but what he retains does not appear to be mixed with material gathered from elsewhere. The wording is often greatly altered, but this comes from the literary style and method of Luke, not from the introduction of fresh documents. Moreover Luke follows the order of Mark in the sections based upon Mark, while Matthew entirely rearranges the order of Mark's anecdotes of the early part of the Galilean Ministry.

These characteristic differences can be expressed in a single sentence. The Gospel according to Matthew is *a fresh edition of Mark*, revised, rearranged, and enriched with new material; the Gospel according to Luke is *a new historical work*, made by combining parts of Mark with parts of other documents.

Generalisations like this have always in them something of over-statement and of paradox. The essential point is, that while the additions to the Marcan framework in Matthew have been combined and altered by the evangelist to fit them into their place in that framework, the non-Marcan matter in Luke has not been combined with the Marcan matter. It would be impossible to reconstruct the first five chapters of Mark out of the Marcan matter preserved in Matthew iii–xiii. 52, although almost every incident and parable is more or less adequately represented,[1] because the anecdotes have been entirely rearranged, and many of them have been interpolated with sayings of Jesus derived from other sources. The non-Marcan material has no doubt been treated in the same way, that is, it has been rearranged and recast by the evangelist. Sayings of Jesus upon cognate topics have been grouped together, whether with the

[1] The exceptions are Mark i. 23–27, 35–39, iii. 9–12, 21, iv. 26–29.

Marcan material, or otherwise (as in the so-called " Sermon on the Mount "), so that we cannot hope to reconstruct the original connexion of this non-Marcan material at all from the position it has come to occupy in the Gospel of Matthew. In the latter part of this Gospel Mark is followed strictly. Hardly anything of any length is omitted, though many fresh collections of sayings and a few fresh incidents, such as the earthquakes at the Death on the Cross and at the appearance of the Angel at the Resurrection, are introduced into the framework of the Marcan narrative. Whatever the origin or value of these additions, they appear in Matthew as additions and enrichments to the main framework; it would be fruitless to endeavour to restore their original context from the use made of them by Matthew.

With the Gospel of Luke it is different. In Luke much of Mark is omitted, and the thread of the Marcan narrative is often dropped altogether. But where Mark is being followed, it is followed to the exclusion of other sources and is generally taken up again almost at the place where it had been dropped.[1] The question therefore

[1] Luke follows Mark throughout five sections of his Gospel, viz.

Luke iv. 31–44	corresponds to	Mark	i. 21–39
v. 12–vi. 19	"	"	i. 40–iii. 19
viii. 4–ix. 50	"	"	iii. 31–ix. 40 (with gaps)
xviii. 15–43	"	"	x. 13–52
xix. 29–xxii. 14	"	"	xi. 1–xiv. 17

In these five sections the only non-Marcan matter is Luke v. 39, xix. 39–44. Much of Mark that falls within the compass of these sections is omitted, viz. Mark iii. 20–30, vi. 1–6, 17–29, vi. 45–viii. 26, x. 35–45, and various bits of xi–xiv. But very little has been dropped at the beginnings and ends of these sections of Luke. Luke v. 12 takes up Mark where it had been left at Luke iv. 44. Only Mark iii. 20–30 is passed over between Luke vi. 19 and viii. 4, and only Mark ix. 41–x. 12 (i. e. 20 verses only) is passed over between Luke ix. 50 and xviii. 15, while nothing of Mark is dropped between Luke xviii. 43 and xix. 29. The only serious transposition of the Marcan matter in these sections is that Mark iii. 31–35 ("Who is my Mother or my Brethren?") is placed after the Parables instead of before them.

naturally arises whether the non-Marcan material in Luke may not have been treated in much the same way, that is to say, that the non-Marcan material stands in Luke in the same order as it stood in the document or documents out of which Luke derived them, and that the thread of it is taken up almost at the places where it has been successively dropped.

It is remarkable how coherent a narrative of our Lord's Ministry we get if we study the non-Marcan material in Luke by itself. In outline it runs as follows: After the Baptism and Temptation Jesus left "Nazara"[1] and came to the Sea of Gennesaret, where Simon Peter became his disciple.[2] We hear of Jesus at Capernaum[3] and at Nain,[4] as he goes "through city and village, bringing the announcement of the

[1] Luke iii–v. 1 ff.; note the spelling *Nazara* in Luke iv. 16, which reappears in Matt. iv. 13.

[2] Luke v. 1 ff. [3] Luke vii. 1. [4] Luke vii. 11.

Kingdom of God, and the Twelve with him and certain women," of whom three are named.[1] Then, "when the days of his ascension were fulfilled, he set his face to go to Jerusalem,"[2] passing Samaritan country on the way,[3] though most of the anecdotes here related still involve a Galilean setting, with synagogues and Pharisees and "multitudes" of hearers.[4] After the parable of the Pharisee and the taxgatherer comes the story of Zacchæus the taxgatherer.[5] So Jesus journeys on, going up to Jerusalem, and when he comes near he weeps over it.[6] Little is said by Luke of the public activity of Jesus in Jerusalem that is not taken from Mark, but we are given a fresh account of the Last Supper,[7] and

[1] Luke viii. 1–4. [2] Luke ix. 51 ff; xiii. 22.

[3] Luke ix. 52, xvii. 11.

[4] Luke xiii. 10, xiv. 1; x. 25, xi. 37, xiii. 31, etc.; xi. 14, xiv. 25, etc.

[5] Luke xviii. 9–14, xix. 1 ff.

[6] Luke xix. 28, 41–44. [7] Luke xxii. 15, 16, 21, 24–38.

much of the Trial of Jesus is independent of Mark, together with nearly all the Lucan account of the Resurrection.

It is as impossible to reconstruct St. Luke's sources from St. Luke's own narrative by the help of our knowledge of his literary methods, as it is to reconstruct Q from the common matter of Matthew and Luke. But it seems to me that we do catch a glimpse of this other source of Luke, especially when we join together, as I think we have a right to do, Luke viii. 1–4 and ix. 51 ff. And then we must ask if this source can be anything else but Q itself?

I doubt very much whether we can get much beyond this stage of queries and uncertainties. But it is well to insist upon the fact of our uncertainty, in order to avoid building pleasing but insecure theories upon unsound literary foundations. Q remains an unknown quantity, for all that some students have begun to treat Harnack's reconstruction of it (or its practical equivalent) as if it had been really discovered, and as if we knew both what it contained and what it left out of the Gospel History.

There are two theories popular at the present time, which seem to me especially insecure : viz., the theory that Q contained no story of the Passion and the theory of the "Peræan Document."

The theory that Q contained no story of the Passion rests on the absence from Matthew, in the Story of the Passion, of any fresh material that reappears in Luke. Assuming this argument to be decisive (as Harnack and others do), and remembering also that Q is no mere collection of Sayings of Jesus, but a document that contained the stories of the Baptism and Temptation of Jesus and of the healing of the Centurion's son—a document moreover which gave prominence to the eschatological hope,[1] we should be forced to the conclusion that it must have been compiled at a very early date, when the first generation of disciples was still living and the Death and Resurrection of the Lord was still not regarded as typical of an experience which all Christians must undergo. This is the stage, to use the striking phrase of Professor Lake, when not "Christ is risen" but *Maranatha* ("Our Lord, come!") was the watchword of Christianity.

But such deductions assume the main theory that the unknown Q had no Passion-story. This still seems to me doubtful: I would sooner believe that the peculiar element in the Lucan Passion-story was derived from Q. It is true that we have in the "Didache" a Christian document that makes much of the watchword *Marana-*

[1] E. g. Luke xii. 35 ff., xvii. 20–37, xxii. 28–30, and the parallels in Matthew.

tha and all that it implies, while it is silent about the Passion. But the "Didache" does not profess to relate the Gospel story at all: I find it difficult to believe that a document like Q, which on any hypothesis goes into some detail about the Ministry of Jesus, could have been silent about the end of his earthly career. Had Q been a mere collection of sayings the silence would have been credible, but we are obliged to allow for the presence of the story of the healing of the Centurion's boy.

And I venture to think that the absence of Lucan parallels in Matthew's story of the Passion is not so very surprising, when we regard the Gospel according to Matthew as what I have called it above; viz., a fresh edition of Mark rather than a new historical work. Many and important as are the additions which Matthew makes to Mark, it is noteworthy that very few of them interrupt the actual course of the narrative. The "Sermon on the Mount" takes three chapters, but in time and place it corresponds to Mark iii. 13. Matthew x. corresponds to Mark vi. 7–11. Mark iv. 33 tells us that "with such parables" Jesus spoke to them the Word; Matthew in chapter xiii. gives half a dozen of these parables. And this is carried out all through the Gospel; the added Sayings of Jesus and the few added anecdotes all slip easily into the Marcan framework. They have been torn from their original context and fitted into Matthew's slightly revised edition of Mark, to serve as illustrations and enrichments. If Q did contain a Passion-story and Matthew made use of it, we need not be surprised to find fragments of it elsewhere than in the Passion-story of Matthew, because Matthew is not combining Q with Mark, but enriching and illustrating Mark from Q and other sources.

For these reasons I think it quite probable that Q had a story of the Passion, and I think it not unlikely that some of it is preserved among the peculiar sections of Luke xxii–xxiv.[1]

The other theory that seems to me hazardous is the identification of the so-called "Peræan" source of Luke. In its crudest form this theory regards the long section, Luke ix. 51–xviii. 14, which corresponds roughly to the single verse Mark x. 1, as giving from some peculiar source an account of the teaching of Jesus during his journey to Jerusalem through Peræa, the country on the other side of Jordan.[2] But much of this section obviously belongs to Q (e. g. ix. 57–61, x. 13–15), and we have seen that its opening words seem to form the continuation of Luke viii. 1–4. It seems

[1] Notably in Luke xxii. 15 f., 24–32, 35–38.

[2] It should be noted that according to Luke our Lord goes through Samaritan villages, and never is represented to have crossed the Jordan at all.

to me impossible to distinguish "Luke's special source," as it is sometimes called, from Q itself, while we must not forget that the unity of the fragments which modern scholars have called Q is still an unproven hypothesis. What was the source from which Luke derived the parables of the Good Samaritan, the Prodigal Son, the Unjust Judge, the Pharisee and the Publican? I fear it must continue to remain uncertain. They have come to us from St. Luke's hands, and we are left to conjecture whence he came to know them, or what amount of rewriting they may have received when he incorporated them into his work.

The plan of this little book does not include a discussion of the historical value of the Fourth Gospel, or of the remarkably divergent stories of the Birth of Christ which form the preface to the Gospel, according to Matthew and Luke. There can be no doubt that the earliest sources for the Life of Jesus are the Gospel of Mark and the source (or sources) which it is convenient to call Q. What has here been attempted has been to vindicate the general historical faithfulness of the picture of our Lord's Ministry sketched in Mark, and to plead for caution in dealing with the unknown Q, a document which the extant evidence does not allow us to reconstruct in detail.

Were the reconstruction of Q possible, were the unlikely to happen and a copy of this long-lost product of primitive Christianity to be dug up by the spade of a modern investigator, it would indeed be a historical jewel of inestimable value. As matters stand, the jewel as a whole is for us irrecoverable, but we have in Matthew and Luke many of the detached gems out of which it was composed. And so much has been said in these pages of the superior historical value of the Gospel of Mark, as compared with those of Matthew and Luke, that it may be well to conclude by pointing out the very considerable degree of faithfulness and historical intelligence which these two evangelists exhibit in essentials, however much the modern investigator may find the naïve and unhellenic narrative of Mark more useful as a basis from which to work.

For the same method,—the comparison of the narrative of Mark as reproduced in Matthew and Luke with the text of Mark itself,—which showed us that we could not reconstruct Mark as a whole from its use by Matthew and Luke, shows at the same time that the parts of Mark which have been so used are retold without essential injury. We stand indeed further off from the scene, and we can no longer discern some characteristic lines in the Portrait of Jesus, when we look at it from the point of view of Matthew or Luke instead of that of Mark; but the figure is the same in essentials. As Matthew and Luke have treated Mark, so no doubt they have treated Q, and if they have retained the essential when they have made use of Mark they will have retained the essential when they have made use of Q.

The very considerable amount of the wording of Mark that Matthew has retained, while it is among the chief pieces of evidence that prove Mark to have been used by him, is also a proof that it has been used with fidelity. But more than this, the general arrangement of the Gospel according to Matthew shows that Mark has been used with intelligence and skill. The divisions of the narrative that Matthew emphasizes are the real turning points. The first part of the Ministry leads up to Peter's confession of Jesus as the Messiah, and the second part, containing the story of the Journey to Jerusalem and the Doctrine of the Cross, starts off at Matthew xvi. 21 with the same formula ("From then began Jesus . . .") as is used in iv. 17 to begin the first part. Much of the matter taken from Mark in the first part has indeed been rearranged, but after all it was little more in the original than a collection of anecdotes. The decisive moment of the open rupture between Jesus and the Pharisees in the Synagogue[1] has been not inappropriately deferred, and it is emphasized after the evangelist's manner by a formal quotation from the Old Testament. In the second part of the Ministry Matthew follows Mark paragraph by paragraph, merely condensing what seemed to be superfluities and adding here and there fresh sayings and legends. Some of the freshness of Mark is gone, and the style has a certain hieratic and set character, which seems like a premonition of future ecclesiastical use. No one can doubt

[1] Matt. xii. 14, corresponding to Mark iii. 6.

that the Gospel of Matthew is better suited than the Gospel of Mark for reading aloud in church. But both tell the same story; the outlines of the picture remain the same. May we not therefore believe that Q was treated with similar intelligence, even though the plan of Matthew did not allow the fragments taken from Q to cohere in their original context?

As we have seen, the plan of the Gospel of Luke is very different from that of Matthew: it is a combination of Mark with other sources rather than an enrichment of Mark from other sources. Much of Mark was dropped altogether in the process, including the general plan of the work. The Ministry of the Christ has become timeless: "the acceptable year of the Lord" is a moment of which the component parts are practically indistinguishable, except that it ends with the arrival at Jerusalem and the Passion; we lose sight of the story told by Mark as a connected whole. But the parts of Mark that are retained are faithfully treated; they are given in their proper order and are very little mixed with other matter. We have therefore some reason for assuming that Luke's other sources have been given in their proper order, without much extraneous mixture. The evangelist indeed professes to write "in order" (Luke i. 3), and judging by his treatment of that one of his sources which we actually possess, this appears to mean that he has preferred to dovetail them together rather than make a new arrangement of their contents.

One special point may be singled out. It has often been noticed that St. Luke's Gospel is eminently the Gospel of women. The Nativity story is told from the woman's point of view: the woman that was a sinner, the women who minister to Jesus, "the daughter of Abraham" who was healed, the "daughters of Jerusalem" who stand on the way to the Crucifixion, the Woman with the Ten Pieces of Silver, the Importunate Widow — all these have come down to us only through the Gospel of Luke. It is therefore worth notice that no sympathetic elaborations are given to the stories of women taken from Mark's Gospel. The stories of Peter's wife's mother, of the Woman with an Issue, and of the Widow's Mites, are repeated in Luke from Mark, but no prominence is given to them; they are, in fact, somewhat curtailed. It seems therefore that the characteristic sympathy given to women and the stress laid upon the women's part in the Ministry of Jesus, belong rather to one or more of Luke's sources than to Luke himself.

However that may be, we cannot doubt that all the sources used by Luke are given by him to us with certain characteristic alterations. His Gospel is like a new building made with old stones: they have been trimmed at the edges to make them fit, or at the least have been repointed with fresh mortar. We can see this for ourselves in the case of the stories taken from Mark, and doubtless the same process has been at work in the others. When Mark gives us the story of the man sick of the palsy, he tells us that it was at Capernaum, that there was a crowd of the inhabitants at the door and that "some of the scribes" were sitting by;[1] in Luke the place is left vague, but sitting by are "Pharisees and Teachers of the Law who had come from every village of Galilee and Judæa and Jerusalem."[2] Cæsarea Philippi and the last visit to Capernaum are not mentioned by Luke. We cannot therefore assume, as has been done by some scholars, that the sources from which Luke drew besides Mark were

[1] Mark ii. 1–6.
[2] Luke v. 17.

themselves destitute of place-names or of indications of time.

It all comes to this, that we can do very little toward reconstructing the unknown sources used by Matthew and Luke, and that we have to depend on the faithfulness and intelligence of these writers, as well as on the excellence of the material they made use of. Our chief guide is the analogy afforded by their use of the Gospel of Mark, which we do possess and which is by far the most valuable source for the Life of Jesus now extant. And those who take in hand to draw up an account of the few decisive months of the public career of Jesus the Nazarene must follow the method rather of the Gospel of Matthew than of the Gospel of Luke. We may attempt to enrich and fill in the bare outline given in Mark, but Mark must remain throughout the basis and foundation of the whole. If the outline given in Mark be not historical, the extant material does not allow us to construct any other.

NOTE ON RECENT RECONSTRUCTIONS OF "Q."

Whether the contents of Q, the "Logian Source," can be safely inferred from a comparison of Matthew and Luke, is a question at issue between scholars, about which sufficient has been already said in these pages. The object of this Note is merely to exhibit in a tabular form two recent attempts at reconstruction, so as to show what kind of document is meant, when Q is named in modern critical discussions.

The two reconstructions are Professor Harnack's ("Sprüche und Reden Jesu," 1907) and Professor Stanton's ("The Gospels as Historical Documents," Part ii, Cambridge, 1909). Harnack constructs Q from 59 or 60 sections of Matthew and Luke, of varying length, and discusses the wording of the several passages in detail; with regard to the position of the more important passages (here numbered by me 1–13) he declares himself practically satisfied.[1] Stanton confines himself almost entirely to the contents of Q, i. e. his reconstruction does not attempt

[1] *Sprüche*, p. 126.

to settle the actual wording of the original document.

In the following Table I give Professor Stanton's eight main divisions, somewhat shortening his titles of the sub-sections, for considerations of space. For the same reason I give only the references to Luke, in the order of which Stanton sees approximately the order of Q (p. 104). The right-hand column contains the corresponding sections of Harnack's Q.

STANTON, pp. 102–103.	HARNACK, p. 126.
I. *The ushering in of the Ministry of Christ.*	
John the Baptist (Luke iii. 3, 7–9, 16 f.).	1*a*
The Baptism (Luke iii. 21 f.).	1*b*
The Temptation (Luke iv. 1–13).	2
II. *The first stage in the preaching of the Gospel.*	
Character of heirs of the Kingdom (Luke vi. 17–49).	3[1]
The Centurion of Capernaum (Luke vii. 1–10).	4
Discourse about the Baptist (Luke vii. 18–28, 31–35).	6

[1] Note that Harnack's 3 is larger than Stanton's II: it includes, for instance, all Stanton's V.

III. *The extension of the Gospel.*

Missionary tour (Luke viii. 1).	[*omitted*]
"Foxes have holes," etc. (Luke ix. 57–60). Harvest plenteous, laborers few (Luke x. 2). Directions to preachers (Luke x. 3–12, 16).	5[1]

IV. *The rejection and the reception of Divine truth.*

"Woe to thee, Chorazin," etc. (Luke x. 13–15).	7
"I thank Thee, Father," etc. (Luke x. 21 f.).	8*a*
"Blessed are your eyes," etc. (Luke x. 23 f.).	(8*b*)

V. *Instruction on Prayer.*

The Lord's Prayer (Luke xi. 2–4). Be earnest in prayer (Luke xi. 9–13).	*parts of* 3

VI. *Jesus and his antagonists.*

The two great commandments (Luke x. 25–28).	[*omitted*]

[1] Harnack's 5 is larger than Stanton's III: see below on VII.

Beelzebub (Luke xi. 14 f., 17–23).
The unclean spirit (Luke xi. 24–26). } 9
The Sign of Jonas (Luke xi. 16, 29–32). 10
The lamp of the body is the eye (Luke xi. 34–36). *part of* 3
"Woe to you, Pharisees!" etc. (Luke xi. 39–52). 11*a*

VII. *Exhortations to disciples in view of the opposition and other trials that awaited them.*

Confess me faithfully (Luke xii. 2–10). *part of* 5
Consider the ravens (Luke xii. 22–34). *part of* 3
The Son of Man coming as a thief (Luke xii. 39 f.).
Act as a prudent steward (Luke xii. 42–46). } 13
Divisions; bear the cross (Luke xii. 51–53, xiv. 26 f.). *part of* 5
Mustard-seed and Leaven (Luke xiii. 18–21). ?
Offences (Luke xvii. 1–4). ?
Faith as a grain of mustard-seed (Luke xvii. 5 f.). ?

VIII. *The doom on Jerusalem and the things of the end.*

"Jerusalem, Jerusalem!" etc. (Luke xiii. 34 f.). 11*b*

The Coming of the Son of Man (Luke xvii. 22–37). 12

The sections marked in the right-hand column with (?) are uncertain in position according to Harnack, but are probably to be inserted very much where Stanton puts them. Stanton's reconstruction of Q does not contain Harnack's § 14, i. e. "He that hath, to him shall be given," followed by the saying in Luke xxii. 28–30 (= Matthew xix. 28) about sitting on twelve thrones judging the twelve tribes of Israel.

BIBLIOGRAPHY

BACON, B. W., *The Beginnings of Gospel Story* (Yale University Press, 1909). [A very suggestive historical Commentary on Mark. The most scientific exposition in English of the anti-eschatological point of view.]

BURKITT, F. C., *The Gospel History and its Transmission* (Edinburgh, 2d ed., 1907). [Attempts to show why the Church preserved an account of the foundation of Christianity which is on the whole historical.]

HARNACK, A., *Lukas der Arzt* (Leipzig, 1906). English translation, *Luke the Physician*, vol. xx of the Crown Theological Library (London and New York, 1907). [A study of Luke, the companion of Paul, and of his writings.]

HARNACK, A., *Sprüche und Reden Jesu* (Leipzig, 1907). English translation, *The Sayings of Jesus*, vol. xxiii of the Crown Theological Library (London and New York, 1908). [The most notable attempt to reconstruct Q.]

HAWKINS, Sir J. C., *Horae Synopticae* (Oxford, 2d ed., 1909). [The best analysis of the peculiarities of the several Synoptic Gospels, the various Tables being arranged with great intelligence as well as accuracy. Invaluable for all investigators of Synoptic problems.]

LAKE, K., *The Historical Evidence for the Resurrection of Jesus Christ*, vol. xxi of the Crown Theological Library (London and New York, 1907). [I introduce this book here as the first example in original English work of the doctrine of the priority of Mark being consistently applied throughout a historical investigation.]

SANDAY, W., *The Life of Christ in Recent Research* (Oxford, 1907). [Lectures, giving a readable survey of the last twenty years of research.]

SCHWEITZER, Albert, *Von Reimarus zu Wrede* (Tübingen, 1906). [The indispensable account of the attempt to write a "Life of Jesus," from the posthumous publication of the tracts of H. S. Reimarus by Lessing in 1778 to that of the late Professor W. Wrede's "Messiah-secret" in 1901. Schweitzer writes from a strongly eschatological point of view. An English translation by W. Montgomery, to be called *The Quest of the Historical Jesus*, will be published in London early in 1910.]

STANTON, V. H., *The Gospels as Historical Documents*, Part II (Cambridge, 1909). [A valuable and very full study of the Synoptic Problem.]

WELLHAUSEN, J., *Einleitung in die drei ersten Evangelien* (Berlin, 1905). — *Das Evangelium Marci* (Berlin, 1903; 2d. ed., 1909). — *Das Evangelium Matthaei* (Berlin, 1904). — *Das Evangelium Lucae* (Berlin, 1904). — [These four books practically form one short Commentary on the Synoptic Gospels, with an Introduction prefixed. The fresh German translations of the Gospels themselves, the running commentary, and the introductory remarks, are all singularly acute and stimulating.]

I cannot close this short Bibliography without remarking that those who wish to study Synoptic questions should prepare themselves by underlining, whether in a Greek or an English New Testament, those words and sentences of Matthew and Luke that are found in Mark. The student should distinguish what is common to all three, what is common to Matthew and Mark only, what is common to

Luke and Mark only, what is common to Matthew and Luke only. There are several "Harmonies" and "Synopses" on the market, some of which are very well arranged. But the grasp of the details of the subject which the student gains by marking the full unabridged texts for himself is worth all the Synopses that ever were compiled.